HILLARY RODHAM CLINTON

❧ HER ESSENTIAL WISDOM ❧

HILLARY RODHAM CLINTON

∿ HER ESSENTIAL WISDOM ∾

EDITED BY
CAROL KELLY-GANGI

FALL RIVER PRESS

New York

FALL RIVER PRESS

New York

An Imprint of Sterling Publishing Co., Inc.
1166 Avenue of the Americas
New York, NY 10036

Compilation © 2018 Carol Kelly-Gangi

ISBN 978-1-4351-6765-0

Distributed in Canada by Sterling Publishing Co., Inc.
c/o Canadian Manda Group, 664 Annette Street
Toronto, Ontario, M6S 2C8, Canada
Distributed in the United Kingdom by GMC Distribution Services
Castle Place, 166 High Street, Lewes, East Sussex, BN7 1XU, England
Distributed in Australia by NewSouth Books
45 Beach Street, Coogee, NSW 2034, Australia

For information about custom editions, special sales, and premium and
corporate purchases, please contact Sterling Special Sales at 800-805-5489
or specialsales@sterlingpublishing.com.

Manufactured in the United States of America

2 4 6 8 10 9 7 5 3

sterlingpublishing.com

Jacket design by David Ter-Avanesyan
Jacket photograph: ZUMA Press, Inc./Alamy

CONTENTS

Introduction ix

Early Years 1

Knowledge, Learning, and Education 7

Government and Democracy 13

America 19

Freedom, Rights, and Justice 27

Equality 33

Activism 39

Women 45

Politics 53

First Lady 63

Foreign Policy 69

The 2016 Presidential Election 77

Religion 89

Hardship and Hope 95

Family and Friendship 103

The Wit and Wisdom of Hillary Clinton. 109

Quotes about Hillary Clinton. 117

Chronology. 129

To my beloved daughter, Emily Grace

INTRODUCTION

When Hillary Rodham Clinton lost her bid in 2016 to become America's first female president, it was a deeply personal loss for millions of Americans. That she garnered close to three million more popular votes was small consolation to the many who struggled to process the shocking outcome. The partisan divide exacerbated by that particularly bruising election only continued afterward. But following Clinton's loss, the country also witnessed a rising tide of activism and engagement, as people young and old, and women in particular, have joined forces to effect change and to make their voices heard.

Clinton has been making her voice heard and fighting for her beliefs for decades. From the start of her public life, she challenged and inspired us with the power and conviction of her words. Clinton is a woman who has literally dedicated her life to public service—as a young lawyer, first lady of Arkansas, First Lady of the United States, senator, secretary of state, and two-time presidential candidate. It is well known that she has also faced more than her fair share of controversy. Indeed, many of her fiercest critics hold firmly onto a skewed and frequently misogynistic caricature that is systematically reinforced by the attack ads and distorted propaganda that has been thrown at her since she first entered the national spotlight as First Lady in the 1990s. But it is Clinton's ability to endure and keep fighting for the America that she knows is stronger together that continues to lift us up in the face of adversity, giving us the hope and optimism to believe that there are brighter days ahead.

Hillary Rodham Clinton: Her Essential Wisdom brings together hundreds of memorable quotations from this remarkable woman. The selections have been carefully collected from her speeches, conferences, debates, and town hall meetings, as well as from her interviews, books, tweets, social media posts, and other writings. Arranged according to theme, the selections reveal the brilliant mind, deep convictions, unwavering determination, as well as the grace and wit that she has exhibited over her extraordinary public life.

In the excerpts, Clinton speaks passionately about America and the American ideals of freedom, equality, and justice, which she has continually striven to promote. She eloquently expresses her commitment to protecting the fundamental human rights and dignity of every person. She shares her fervent belief in the need for quality education for every child. In other excerpts, she reveals her keen insights into foreign policy and her vision for the role that America should play on the world stage. Of course, there is also a sampling of selections about her decades in politics, and especially from and about the 2016 presidential election—sharing both her frustrations and the insights she has gained.

Elsewhere, we see a more personal side of Clinton. She lovingly recalls her parents, and how they each guided and challenged her in very different ways. She speaks of her steadfast love for her husband, Bill Clinton, despite the challenges they have faced in their life together. She shares the pride and joy she feels for her daughter,

Chelsea, and now her grandchildren, and how her deep faith has informed her life. There is a chapter that contains a glimpse of the keen wit and practical wisdom that is all her own. And the final chapter gathers quotations about Hillary Clinton in which politicians, writers, feminists, heads of state, political rivals, and members of her family share their insights into Hillary the person, her complexities, and her legacy.

Hillary Rodham Clinton: Her Essential Wisdom invites readers to experience the powerful words of this remarkable woman and leader, who continues to inspire and challenge so many of us in this great nation and in the world.

—CAROL KELLY-GANGI
2018

EARLY YEARS

She never let me back down from any challenge. When I tried to hide from a neighborhood bully, she literally blocked the door. "Go back out there," she said.

—About her mother, Dorothy Rodham, during acceptance speech,
Democratic National Convention, Philadelphia, July 28, 2016

By the time I was twelve, I had my own positions on many issues. I also learned that a person was not necessarily bad just because you did not agree with him, and that if you believed in something, you had better be prepared to defend it.

—*Living History*

When I brought home straight A's from junior high, my father's only comment was, "Well, Hillary, that must be an easy school you go to." By raising the bar, he encouraged me to study even harder, and in fact, comments like that spurred me on.

—*It Takes a Village*

There was no distinction between me and my brothers or any barriers thrown up to me that I couldn't think about something because I was a girl. If you work hard enough and you really apply yourself then you should be able to do whatever you choose to do.

—*Hillary Rodham Clinton: A First Lady for Our Time*,
by Donnie Radcliffe

My family, like every family I know of, was far from perfect. But however imperfect we were, as individuals and as a unit, we were bound together by a sense of commitment and security. My mother and father did what parents do best: They dedicated their time, energy, and money to their children and made sacrifices to give us a better life.

—*It Takes a Village*

We didn't trust government, authority figures, or really anyone over thirty, in large part thanks to years of heavy casualties and dishonest official statements about Vietnam, and deep differences over civil rights and poverty here at home. We were asking urgent questions about whether women, people of color, religious minorities, immigrants, would ever be treated with dignity and respect.

—Commencement address,
Wellesley College, May 26, 2017

There's a very strange conservative strain that goes through a lot of New Left, collegiate protests that I find very intriguing because it harkens back to a lot of the old virtues, to the fulfillment of original ideas. And it's also a very unique American experience. It's such a great adventure. If the experiment in human living doesn't work in this country, in this age, it's not going to work anywhere.

—Commencement address as senior class spokesman,
Wellesley College, May 31, 1969

[S]ome of the men were just rattling us, [saying,] "What are you doing here? You shouldn't be here." "You're taking a place of a man who could maybe get drafted and die in Vietnam." It was just really personal! Personal and pointed.

—Recalling her experience waiting to take the law school admissions test, *Glamour*, August 2014

❧

But I had to learn as a young woman to control my emotions. And that's a hard path to walk. Because you need to protect yourself, you need to keep steady, but at the same time you don't want to seem "walled off."

—Post, *Humans of New York*
September 8, 2016

❧

I noticed that he kept looking over at me. He had been doing a lot of that. So I stood up from the desk, walked over to him and said, "If you're going to keep looking at me, and I'm going to keep looking back, we might as well be introduced. I'm Hillary Rodham." That was it.

—*Living History*

In one of those strange twists of fate that enters all our lives if we're open to hear and see them, I knew right away that I had to go to work for her.

—On deciding to work with Marian Wright Edelman at the Children's Defense Fund, "The Rising Lawyer's Detour to Arkansas," *Washington Post*, January 12, 1993

KNOWLEDGE, LEARNING, AND EDUCATION

We also know that to be educated, the goal of it must be human liberation. A liberation enabling each of us to fulfill our capacity so as to be free to create within and around ourselves.

—**Commencement address as senior class spokesman,
Wellesley College, May 31, 1969**

Sparking someone's love of learning, changing the course of a life, standing up for the freedom to read, to learn. Nothing is more important than that in a free society.

—**Speech, American Library Association Annual Conference,
Chicago, June 27, 2017**

I've been a champion for early childhood education for as long as I can remember, really starting when I was in law school and got interested in, as I was studying the law, why do some people follow the law and other people don't? What's in their background? What makes them either a productive member of society or somebody on the outside who may be trying to tear down instead of build up?

—**Campaign speech, Rochester, New Hampshire, June 15, 2015**

Every child in this country deserves a good teacher, in a good school—regardless of the zip code that child lives in.

—*Stronger Together*

I do believe with all my heart that everything we need to do in our country really starts with how we treat our children and how we try to raise them, taking care of their needs, being able to stimulate them, to give them a better chance in life, helping them become successful and good citizens.

—Campaign speech, Rochester, New Hampshire, June 15, 2015

We need libraries and librarians now more than ever. . . . [R]eading changes lives. Whether it's old-fashioned books or e-readers, wherever it is. I can remember the first time I got a library card. I was so excited. As a little girl I was always reading something, from *Nancy Drew* to *Little Women* to James Michener, and when I got that library card, it felt like I'd been handed a passport to the world.

—Speech, American Library Association Annual Conference, Chicago, June 27, 2017

There's a lot of turmoil within public education, and I am a stalwart supporter of public education. I think it still remains one of the foundational institutions of our democracy, so I don't want to see it be discredited, undermined, dismissed in any way. We have got to have early-childhood education, especially starting with low-income, disadvantaged kids, if we're going to prepare kids to succeed when they get to elementary school.

—Interview, *Newsday* editorial board, April 11, 2016

We know when girls have equal opportunities to primary and secondary school, cycles of poverty are broken, economies grow, glass ceilings are cracked, and potential unleashed.

—"Equality for Girls and Women: 2034 Instead of 2134?"
plenary session, Clinton Global Initiative,
New York City, September 2014

∽

America is asking more of our educators than ever before. We look to them to fill in gaps that we as a country have neglected. . . . And we ask them to help right wrongs—from poverty and homelessness to the legacy of racial inequities stretching back centuries. We ask so much of our teachers—and we don't give them enough in return.

—*Stronger Together*

∽

No government can love a child, and no policy can substitute for a family's care. But at the same time, government can either support or undermine families as they cope with moral, social, and economic stresses of caring for children.

—Remarks as First Lady, Child Welfare League
seventy-fifth anniversary dinner,
Washington, D.C., March 1, 1995

We need to educate our children for the future, not the past. We want our children to be creators, innovators, and entrepreneurs—critical thinkers who can collaborate and communicate within their communities and around the world.

—Stronger Together

❧

[T]oo often, training and retraining doesn't work as it should. If you don't have a four-year degree, if you haven't really had the chance to upgrade your skills over the years, it's hard to just make a course correction. We need to have apprenticeships and community college and technical programs, starting in high school and moving all the way up to older workers. Whether you're trying to start your career or you've spent decades contributing to our economy, you deserve better.

**—Campaign speech, Frontline Outreach Center, Orlando, Florida,
September 21, 2016**

GOVERNMENT
AND DEMOCRACY

The first priority of any government is to protect and ensure the safety of its citizens.

—Keynote address, eighty-first annual Hannukah dinner,
Yeshiva University, December 4, 2005

In a democracy, government is the people, so renewing our faith in our government means renewing our faith in ourselves and in our ability to perfect our union.

—Commencement address, Drew University, May 18, 1996

Democracies protect and respect citizens every day, not just on Election Day. And democracies demonstrate their greatness not by insisting they are perfect, but by using their institutions and their principles to make themselves—and their union—"more perfect," just as our country continues to do after 233 years.

—Speech as secretary of state, Georgetown University,
December 14, 2009

Our Founders fought a revolution and wrote a constitution so America would never be a nation where one person had all the power. Two hundred and forty years later, we still put our faith in each other.

—Acceptance speech, Democratic National Convention,
Philadelphia, July 28, 2016

Whether you're on the right or the left, you cannot believe you have the only truth. That's not the way a democracy works. That's not the way our country has succeeded. You have to listen to each other, and yes, you have to find compromise.

—*The Today Show*, October 12, 2011

Governments are responsible for promoting disciplined economic politics. They must strengthen the conditions that sustain democracy and market economies that we know can unleash the creative energies of millions of people—if these people are prepared to take advantage of the opportunities available to them.

—Sixth CNN World Report Conference, Atlanta, May 2, 1995

[I]t is only civil society that can inculcate the values of democracy, those habits of the heart. It is only through our families, our religious organizations, our associations at the civic and the neighborhood level, our trade unions, our other groups where we come together voluntarily joining in forums to create better opportunities that we will really create democracy.

—Remarks as First Lady, Women in Democracy Conference, Vienna, July 11, 1997

What's great about our political system is that we are all judged on our own merits.

—**Democratic presidential primary debate, Los Angeles, January 31, 2008**

❧

There cannot be true democracy unless women's voices are heard. There cannot be true democracy unless women are given the opportunity to take responsibility for their own lives. There cannot be true democracy unless all citizens are able to participate fully in the lives of their country.

—**Remarks as First Lady, Women in Democracy Conference, Vienna, July 11, 1997**

❧

I do believe that, based on my experience in the Senate, based on my work as secretary of state, women decision-makers see issues from our own perspective, our own different sets of experiences, and are more open to different kinds of solutions that we then can link to our experience. So I think that there is a difference in governing.

—**Interview, *Newsday* editorial board, April 11, 2016**

The worst thing that can happen in a democracy—as well as in an individual's life—is to become cynical about the future and lose hope.

—Comments, African American Leadership Summit,
Washington, D.C., as quoted in "Hillary's Last Chance,"
Esquire, January 29, 2007

Our constitutional democracy enshrines the peaceful transfer of power. We don't just respect that. We cherish it. It also enshrines other things: the rule of law, the principle that we are all equal in rights and dignity, freedom of worship and expression. We respect and cherish these values too, and we must defend them.

—Concession speech, presidential election,
New York City, November 9, 2016

AMERICA

Dr. King told us our lives begin to end the day we become silent about things that matter. Well, I'm here to tell you poverty and growing inequality matters. Health care matters. The people of the Gulf Coast and New Orleans matter. Our soldiers matter. Our standing in the world matters. Our future matters. And it is up to us to take it back, put it in to our hands, start marching toward a better tomorrow!

—**Remarks, forty-second anniversary of Selma-to-Montgomery March, Alabama, March 4, 2007**

❧

We Americans have a long tradition of being engaged in the broader community. As we kept pressing back the frontiers of this new nation, Americans began forming all kinds of informal associations and institutions—our churches, and civic organizations, and business groups—filled with people who were working not only to build a better future for themselves, but for others as well. When a barn needed to be raised—or a school roof needed to be repaired—everyone pitched in. That's always been the key to our strong and vibrant civil society—and the bedrock of our democracy.

—**Commencement address, Howard University, 1998**

❧

I believe that the foundation of a strong economy doesn't begin with giving people who are already privileged and wealthy even more benefits. I think it comes from shared prosperity.

—**Speech as senator, Take Back America 2007 Conference, June 20, 2007**

In America, if you can dream it, you should be able to build it. We're going to help you balance family and work. And you know what? If fighting for affordable child care and paid family leave is playing the "woman card," then deal me in.

—*Acceptance speech, Democratic National Convention, Philadelphia, July 28, 2016*

We have to heal the divides in our country. Not just on guns, but on race, immigration, and more. That starts with listening to each other, hearing each other, trying, as best we can, to walk in each other's shoes.

—Acceptance speech, Democratic National Convention,
Philadelphia, July 28, 2016

I believe with all my heart that America is an exceptional country—that we're still, in Lincoln's words, the last, best hope of earth. We are not a country that cowers behind walls. We lead with purpose, and we prevail.

—Campaign speech on national security,
San Diego, June 2, 2016

We've spent a year and a half bringing together millions of people from every corner of our country to say with one voice that we believe that the American dream is big enough for everyone—for people of all races and religions, for men and women, for immigrants, for LGBT people, and people with disabilities. For everyone.

—Concession speech, presidential election,
New York City, November 9, 2016

America's strength doesn't come from lashing out. Strength relies on smarts, judgment, cool resolve, and the precise and strategic application of power.

—**Acceptance speech, Democratic National Convention,
Philadelphia, July 28, 2016**

❧

I love our country. I believe in the American people. I know what we are capable of. Throughout history, generations of Americans have risen together to meet the tests of their time. They defended democracy, built the greatest middle class that the world has ever seen, marched for civil rights and voting rights, for workers' rights and women's rights, LGBT rights, and rights for people with disabilities.

—**Campaign speech, University of Pittsburgh,
November 7, 2016**

❧

[F]or as long as America has existed, it has been the American way to reject can't-do claims and to choose instead to stretch the boundaries of the possible through hard work, determination, and a pioneering spirit.

—**Concession speech, Democratic presidential primary,
Washington, D.C., June 7, 2008**

Are we going to reconfirm the promise of America, which does have a place for immigrants, which does try to move people to being more unified and not divisive, that does expect leaders to bring people together, not tear them apart? Are we going to chart a course in keeping with our history? Because I think we already are great, but there's no guarantee we stay great unless we work together, leaders and citizens alike.

—Campaign interview with Chris Cuomo, CNN,
Park Ridge, Illinois, May 19, 2016

Finally, I am so grateful for our country and for all it has given to me. I count my blessings every single day that I am an American. And I still believe, as deeply as I ever have, that if we stand together and work together with respect for our differences, strength in our convictions, and love for this nation, our best days are still ahead of us.

—Concession speech, presidential election,
New York City, November 9, 2016

We have the most dynamic and diverse people in the world. We have the most tolerant and generous young people we've ever had. We have the most powerful military and the most innovative entrepreneurs.

—Acceptance speech, Democratic National Convention,
Philadelphia, July 28, 2016

To be great, we can't be small. We have to be as big as the values that define America. And we are a big-hearted, fair-minded country. We teach our children that this is one nation under God, indivisible, with liberty and justice for all. Not just for people who look a certain way or worship a certain way or love a certain way. For all. Indivisible.

—**Victory speech as presumptive Democratic presidential nominee,**
Brooklyn, June 7, 2016

Pass Hate Crimes Legislation Now!

www.unitedagainsthate.org

FREEDOM, RIGHTS, AND JUSTICE

We have the most enduring values—freedom and equality, justice and opportunity. We should be proud that those words are associated with the United States of America.

—Acceptance speech, Democratic National Convention,
Philadelphia, July 28, 2016

❧

Freedom means the right of people to assemble, organize, and debate openly. It means respecting the views of those who may disagree with the views of their governments. It means not taking citizens away from their loved ones and jailing them, mistreating them, or denying them their freedom or dignity because of peaceful expression of their ideas and opinions.

—Remarks as First Lady, United Nations Fourth World Conference
on Women, Beijing, September 5, 1995

❧

The very idea that in the twenty-first century, African-Americans would wait in line for ten hours [to vote] while whites in an affluent precinct next to theirs waited in line for ten minutes, or that African-Americans would receive flyers telling them the wrong time and day to exercise their constitutional right to vote. That's wrong. It is simply unconscionable that today young Americans are putting their lives at risk to protect democracy half a world away when here at home their precious right to vote is under siege.

—Remarks, forty-second anniversary of Selma-to-Montgomery March,
Alabama, March 4, 2007

It does not matter what country we live in, who our leaders are or even who we are. Because we are human, we therefore have rights. And because we have rights, governments are bound to protect them.

—Speech as secretary of state, International Human Rights Day, Geneva, December 6, 2011

Human rights have both negative and positive requirements. People should be free from tyranny in whatever form, and they should also be free to seize the opportunities of a full life.

—Speech as secretary of state, Georgetown University, December 14, 2009

Americans believe that the desire for dignity and self-determination is universal, and we do try to act on that belief around the world. Americans have fought and died for these ideals. And when freedom gains ground anywhere, Americans are inspired.

—Keynote address, National Democratic Institute's 2011 Democracy Awards Dinner, Washington, D.C., November 7, 2011

It goes to the heart of who we are as women, our rights, our autonomy, our ability to make our own decisions, and we need to be talking about that and defending Planned Parenthood from these outrageous attacks.

—Democratic presidential primary debate, New York City, April 14, 2016

Voting is the most precious right of every citizen, and we have a moral obligation to ensure the integrity of our voting process.

—**Remarks as U.S. senator about Election Reform Bill,**
September 30, 2005

❧

So, my hope now, today, is that whatever our disagreements with those in this debate, that we join together to take real action to improve the quality of health care for women and families, to reduce the number of abortions and to build a healthier, brighter, more hopeful future for women and girls in our country and around the world.

—**Speech marking thirty-second anniversary of** *Roe v. Wade,*
New York State Family Planning Providers,
Albany, New York, January 24, 2005

❧

I will defend Roe v. Wade, and I will defend women's rights to make their own health care decisions. We have come too far to have that turn back now.

—**Final presidential debate, University of Nevada,**
Las Vegas, October 20, 2016

❧

Everything I have seen has convinced me that life is freer, fairer, healthier, safer, and far more humane when women are empowered to make their own reproductive health decisions.

—**Speech, Planned Parenthood, Washington, D.C.,**
June 10, 2016

This is one of the worst possible choices that any woman and her family has to make. And I do not believe the government should be in it. I've been to countries where governments forced women to have abortions like they did in China, or force women to bear children like they used to do in Romania. I can tell: You the government has no business in the decisions that women make with their families in accordance with their faith, with medical advice, and I will stand up for that right.

—**Final presidential debate, University of Nevada,
Las Vegas, October 20, 2016**

I think when we talk about the Supreme Court, it really raises the central issue in this election—namely, what kind of country are we going to be? What kind of opportunities will we provide for our citizens? What kind of rights will Americans have? And I feel strongly that the Supreme Court needs to stand on the side of the American people, not on the side of the powerful corporations and the wealthy.

—**Final presidential debate, University of Nevada,
Las Vegas, October 20, 2016**

For all the injustices in our past and our present, we have to believe that in the free exchange of ideas, justice will prevail over injustice, tolerance over intolerance and progress over reaction.

—**Commencement speech as First Lady,
University of Pennsylvania, May 17, 1993**

EQUALITY

St. Paul told us, in the letter to the Galatians, "Let us not grow weary in doing good, for in due seasons we shall reap, if we do not lose heart." The brave men and women of Bloody Sunday did not lose heart. We can do no less. We have a march to finish. Let us join together and complete that march for freedom, justice, opportunity, and everything America should be.

—Remarks, forty-second anniversary of Selma-to-Montgomery March, Alabama, March 4, 2007

Despite our founding principles and the many ways our constitution has protected individual liberties, we do, let's admit it, have a long history of shutting people out—African Americans, women, gays and lesbians, people with disabilities—and throughout our history, we have found too many ways to divide and exclude people from their ownership of the law and protection under the law.

—Acceptance speech, 2013 ABA Medal, American Bar Association Annual Meeting, San Francisco, August 12, 2013

We feel so passionately about this because we are not only running for office, but we each, in our own way, have lived it. We have seen it. We have understood the pain and the injustice that has come because of race, because of gender.

—Democratic presidential primary debate, Myrtle Beach, South Carolina, January 21, 2008

I bring the experiences of women. As a daughter, as a mother, as a wife, as a sister. That is who I am. Those experiences are part of me. And it is part of our American journey that we have moved through so much of what used to hold people back because of gender, because of race. Are we there yet? Is the journey over? I don't think so, and I don't think any fair person would say that.

—Interview with Tim Russert, *Meet the Press*, January 13, 2008

Every social movement, every economic advance has only come about because people were willing to work and sacrifice and keep pushing forward in the face of adversity. It's not easy. It wasn't easy to get the vote for women. It wasn't easy to have the final efforts made to ensure that the Civil Rights Act was enforced. It wasn't easy because there are powerful interests still trying to push us back and push us down.

—Campaign speech, Coastal Credit Union Music Park,
Raleigh, North Carolina, November 3, 2016

I want white people to recognize that there is systemic racism. It's also in employment, it's in housing, but it is in the criminal justice system, as well.

—Democratic presidential primary debate,
Brooklyn, New York, April 14, 2016

We know their names: Trayvon Martin and Eric Garner and Sandra Bland and Keith Scott and so many others. We have got to face this, and we're going to get to work to do just that. We are going to . . . dismantle the so-called school-to-prison pipeline, and we're going to replace it with a cradle-to-college pipeline.

—**Campaign speech, Raleigh, North Carolina,**
November 3, 2016

❧

Prediction from a grown-up: You're future is going to be amazing. You will surprise yourself with what you're capable of and the incredible things you go on to do. Find the people who love and believe in you. There will be lots of them.

—**Offering words of encouragement to a gay teen anxious**
about his future, Facebook, July 3, 2015

❧

My views did evolve, and I think most people my age would say the same thing. There might be some exceptions, but largely because of my strong opposition to discrimination of any sort and my personal relationships with a lot of people over the years, I certainly concluded that marriage equality should be the law of the land, and I was thrilled when the Supreme Court made it the law of the land.

—**Campaign town hall meeting, Keene, New Hampshire, October 2015**

Gay rights are human rights.

—Speech as secretary of state, International Human Rights Day,
Geneva, December 6, 2011

Being gay is not a Western invention; it is a human reality. And
protecting the human rights of all people, gay or straight, is not
something that only Western governments do. . . .

—Speech as secretary of state, International Human Rights Day,
Geneva, December 6, 2011

To LGBT men and women worldwide, let me say this: Wherever
you live and whatever the circumstances of your life, whether you are
connected to a network of support or feel isolated and vulnerable, please
know that you are not alone.

—Speech as secretary of state, International Human Rights Day,
Geneva, December 6, 2011

We need to imagine what it's like to walk in each other's shoes. We
need to begin to understand what it's like to be a young black man or
a Muslim American or a first-generation Latino American or a police
officer. . . . Finding solutions challenges us to dig deep and constantly
seek the right balance. But our country succeeds when all of us share
in the promise of America—no matter who you are, what you look
like, where you come from, or who you love.

—*Stronger Together*

CLINTON GLOBAL INITIATIVE

ACTIVISM

Way back when I was in college, and I gave the commencement speech, I said to my classmates then that our goal should be to make what appears to be impossible possible. I may be older now, a mother and a grandmother. I have seen my share of ups and downs, but I still believe that we can make the impossible possible.

—Speech, Children's Defense Fund Gala,
Washington, D.C., November 16, 2016

∽

I didn't get into public service to hold high office. Forty-five years ago, that would have seemed an absolute incredibly wrong-headed view, but I did decide to be an activist to use my law degree to help kids. Every child deserves to have the opportunity to live up to his or her God-given potential, and I believe the measure of any society is how we treat our children.

—Speech, Children's Defense Fund Gala,
Washington, D.C., November 16, 2016

∽

[A]s a senator, I helped to rebuild New York City after 9/11 and provided health care to our brave first responders. As your secretary of state, I traveled to one hundred twelve countries, negotiated cease-fires, reduced the threat of nuclear weapons, stood up for human rights and women's rights and LGBT rights all around the world.

—Campaign speech, Raleigh, North Carolina,
November 3, 2016

I started my career fighting for children and families with the Children's Defense Fund when I [finished] law school in the 1970s. I went to South Carolina to gather evidence to stop the government in South Carolina from putting young men, teenagers in jails with adults. I went to Alabama undercover to gather information about segregated academies to deprive them of tax-exempt status, which they did not deserve. I went door to door in New Bedford, Massachusetts, gathering information to make the case that every child in America, including children with disabilities, should have the right to a public school education.

—Campaign speech, Raleigh, North Carolina,
November 3, 2016

All of us respond to children. We want to nurture them so they can dream the dreams that free and healthy children should have. This is our primary responsibility as adults.

—Remarks as First Lady, American Medical Association,
Chicago, June 13, 1993

Four hundred pieces of legislation have my name on it as a sponsor or co-sponsor when I was a senator for eight years. I worked very hard and was proud to be reelected in New York by an even bigger margin than I had been elected the first time.

—Second presidential debate, Washington University, St. Louis,
October 9, 2016

Let's be clear: When I talk about children in or near poverty, this isn't someone else's problem. These aren't someone else's children. This is America's problem, because they are America's children.

—*Speech, Children's Defense Fund Gala, Washington, D.C., November 16, 2016*

So, it's true. I sweat the details of policy—whether we're talking about the exact level of lead in the drinking water in Flint, Michigan, the number of mental health facilities in Iowa, or the cost of your prescription drugs. Because it's not just a detail if it's your kid—if it's your family. It's a big deal. And it should be a big deal to your president, too.

—Acceptance speech, Democratic National Convention,
Philadelphia, July 28, 2016

~

I'm thrilled to talk about the Clinton Foundation, because it is a world-renowned charity and I'm so proud of the work that it does. . . . [T]he Clinton Foundation made it possible for eleven million people around the world with HIV-AIDS to afford treatment, and that's about half of all the people in the world that are getting treatment in partnership with the American Health Association.

—Final presidential debate,
University of Nevada, Las Vegas, October 20, 2016

~

What I try to do every day is figure out how to help somebody. You can't always pass the laws you want to pass right away. You can't snap your fingers and get people to cooperate. You have to work on that every minute of every day. But you can try to help somebody every single day. I have tried to do that as a public servant, as an activist, and now as a senator, and that's what I will do as president.

—Campaign speech, Johnston, Iowa,
December 17, 2007

WOMEN

If there is one message that echoes forth from this conference, it is that human rights are women's rights, and women's rights are human rights. Let us not forget that among those rights are the right to speak freely. And the right to be heard.

—Remarks as First Lady, United Nations Fourth World Conference on Women, Beijing, September 5, 1995

But we know that it takes strength to keep your voice heard. We know that it takes courage to stand up for those without voices. All of you who tore down communism did so because you believed in democracy and freedom and the human heart and spirit. Now you fight for women's rights because you believe in the same values. One barrier is rubble; the other is crumbling.

—Remarks as First Lady, Women in Democracy Conference, Vienna, July 11, 1997

Women have always been the primary victims of war. Women lose their husbands, their fathers, their sons in combat. Women often have to flee from the only homes they have ever known. Women are often the refugees from conflict and sometimes, more frequently in today's warfare, victims. Women are often left with the responsibility, alone, of raising the children.

—Remarks, First Ladies' Conference on Domestic Violence, San Salvador, El Salvador, November 17, 1998

Women are the largest untapped reservoir of talent in the world.
. . . It is past time for women to take their rightful place, side by
side with men, in the rooms where the fates of peoples, where their
children's and grandchildren's fates, are decided . . .

—Keynote address as secretary of state, International
Crisis Group's "In Pursuit of Peace" Award Dinner,
New York City, December 16, 2011

There's that kind of double bind that women find themselves in.
On the one hand, yes, be smart, stand up for yourself. On the other
hand, don't offend anybody, don't step on toes, or you'll become
somebody that nobody likes because you're too assertive.

—"The Real Hillary Clinton," *Midwest Today*,
June 1994

Although we weren't able to shatter that highest, hardest glass
ceiling this time, thanks to you, it's got about 18 million cracks
in it, and the light is shining through like never before, filling us
all with the hope and the sure knowledge that the path will be a
little easier next time.

—Concession speech, 2008 Democratic presidential primary,
Washington, D.C., June 7, 2008

We need to understand that there is no formula for how women should lead their lives. That is why we must respect the choices that each woman makes for herself and her family. Every woman deserves the chance to realize her God-given potential.

—**Remarks as First Lady, United Nations Fourth World Conference on Women, Beijing, September 5, 1995**

❧

Tonight, we've reached a milestone in our nation's march toward a more perfect union: the first time that a major party has nominated a woman for president. Standing here, standing here as my mother's daughter, and my daughter's mother, I'm so happy this day has come. I'm happy for grandmothers and little girls and everyone in between. I'm happy for boys and men, too—because when any barrier falls in America, for anyone, it clears the way for everyone. After all, when there are no ceilings, the sky's the limit. So, let's keep going—let's keep going until every one of the 161 million women and girls across America has the opportunity she deserves to have.

—**Acceptance speech, Democratic National Convention, Philadelphia, July 28, 2016**

❧

To every little girl who dreams big: Yes, you can be anything you want—even president.

—**@HillaryClinton, Twitter, June 7, 2016**

When that day arrives, and a woman takes the oath of office as our president, we will all stand taller, proud of the values of our nation, proud that every little girl can dream big and that her dreams can come true in America.

—Concession speech, 2008 Democratic presidential primary, Washington, D.C., June 7, 2008

I challenge assumptions about women. I do make some people uncomfortable, which I'm well aware of, but that's just part of coming to grips with what I believe is still one of the most important pieces of unfinished business in human history— empowering women to be able to stand up for themselves.

—"Her Brilliant Career," *Vogue*, December 2009

I've had the great privilege of traveling around the world, visiting in many different settings far from the formal palaces or offices where leaders are, but into villages, down dusty roads, meeting with people. . . . And there is still so much inequity, so much unfairness, so much disrespect and discrimination toward women and girls.

—Interview with Christiane Amanpour, Women for Women International Luncheon, New York City, May 2, 2017

To all the little girls who are watching this, never doubt that you are valuable and powerful and deserving of every chance and opportunity in the world to pursue and achieve your own dreams.

—Concession speech, United States presidential election,
New York City, November 9, 2016

❧

But I also think I may have underestimated the staying power of sexism and particularly the disparity in treatment not just in politics but in all kinds of businesses and academia and society at large.

—"Exclusive: Hillary Clinton Says Trump Associates
Helped Russia Meddle in the 2016 Election,"
USA Today, September 11, 2017

❧

Speak your opinion more fervently in your classes if you're a student, or at meetings in your workplace. Proudly take credit for your ideas. Have confidence in the value of your contributions. And if the space you're in doesn't have room for your voice, don't be afraid to carve out a space of your own.

—*The Toast* blog, July 1, 2016

I have always believed that women are not victims. We are agents of change. We are drivers of progress. We are makers of peace. All we need is a fighting chance.

—*Remarks as former secretary of state,*
Women in the World Summit,
New York City, April 5, 2013

POLITICS

I think that people who are married to politicians are under a tremendous strain, because unless you have a pretty strong sense of your own self-identity, it becomes very easy to be buffeted about by all the people who are around your husband.

—*In Focus*, KAIT-TV, Jonesboro, Arkansas, 1979

∾

I suppose I could have stayed home and baked cookies and had teas, but what I decided to do was to fulfill my profession, which I entered before my husband was in public life.

—Responding to reporters' questions at a campaign stop, Chicago, March 16, 1992

∾

I have learned over the last many years, being involved in politics, and especially since my husband first started running for president, that the best thing to do in these cases is just to be patient, take a deep breath and the truth will come out. But there's nothing we can do to fight this fire storm of allegations that are out there.

—Commenting on the Monica Lewinsky scandal, *The Today Show*, January 27, 1998

[T]he great story here for anybody willing to find it, write about it and explain it is this vast right-wing conspiracy that has been conspiring against my husband since the day he announced for president.

—Interview with Matt Lauer,
The Today Show, January 27, 1998

❧

I've gone from a Barry Goldwater Republican to a New Democrat, but I think my underlying values have remained pretty constant: individual responsibility and community—I don't see those as mutually inconsistent.

—"Hillary's Turn," *New York*, April 3, 2000

❧

[T]his is more like a return to what I had done before those eight years {as First Lady}. It has a definition; it has responsibilities. There are certain things you are expected to do. You do them to the best of your ability. So I'm very comfortable having this job . . .

—"The Student: How Hillary Clinton Set Out to Master the Senate,"
The New Yorker, October 13, 2003

❧

I learned some valuable lessons about the legislative process, the importance of bipartisan cooperation and the wisdom of taking small steps to get a big job done.

—Clinton's first address on the floor of the Senate,
via CNN, February 14, 2001

I think part of the reason . . . there's so much intensity in this
campaign is that [Senator Barack Obama and I] have a lot of mutual
supporters. We have people who would be one hundred percent for
either of us were the other not in the race.

—Interview with Bob Schieffer,
Face the Nation, January 27, 2008

This is an exciting and historic campaign. One of us is going to make
history, which is thrilling to me. I've worked all my life on behalf
of civil rights and women's rights and human rights, and so I want
a good, vigorous campaign about the differences between us and
our various qualifications and experiences to be the president that
America needs.

—Interview with Tim Russert,
Meet the Press, January 13, 2008

I am very, very proud of my husband's record as a leader in our
country going back so many years, and what he's done. And people
know his heart. They know . . . what he has stood for. So, I'm really
glad that he's there with me.

—Commenting on Bill Clinton's support of her candidacy,
interview with Bob Schieffer, *Face the Nation*,
January 27, 2008

I have been through these Republican attacks over and over and over again, and I believe that I've demonstrated that, much to the dismay of the Republicans, I not only can survive, but thrive.

—**Interview with George Stephanopoulos,**
***This Week*, February 3, 2008**

ص

Being a serious candidate for president as a woman brought out all the stuff that still exists about that. Some of it was personal, some of it was gender based, and you kind of accept it. I think that if you live long enough, you realize that so much of what happens in life is out of your control, but how you respond to it is in your control. That's what I try to remember.

—**"Hillary Clinton: Myth & Reality,"**
***Harper's Bazaar*, February 14, 2011**

ص

The way to continue our fight now, to accomplish the goals for which we stand, is to take our energy, our passion, our strength, and do all we can to help elect Barack Obama the next president of the United States. Today, as I suspend my campaign, I congratulate him on the victory he has won and the extraordinary race he has run. I endorse him and throw my full support behind him. And I ask all of you to join me in working as hard for Barack Obama as you have for me.

—**Concession speech, Democratic presidential primary,**
Washington, D.C., June 7, 2008

I ran a really hard campaign against President Obama, all through 2008. And we went all the way to the end, all the way into June. I actually ended up with slightly more votes, but he ended up with more delegates, and I withdrew. I endorsed him. I nominated him at the convention and I worked very hard to get him elected. It was not easy.

—Interview, *Newsday* editorial board, April 11, 2016

A political life, I've often said, is a continuing education in human nature, including one's own. My involvement on the ground floor of two presidential campaigns and my duties as First Lady took me to every state in our union and to seventy-eight nations. In each place, I met someone or saw something that caused me to open my mind and my heart and deepen my understanding of the universal concerns that most of humanity shares.

—*Living History*

Look, I do think that I am somebody who is perhaps more private, more—not for bad reasons. It's just my personality. It's just my temperament.

—"Politico's Glenn Thrush Interviews Hillary Clinton," *Politico*, April 6, 2016

The truth is, through all these years of public service, the "service" part has always come easier to me than the "public" part.

—**Acceptance speech, Democratic National Convention,**
Philadelphia, July 28, 2016

❧

I am not a natural politician, in case you haven't noticed, unlike my husband or President Obama. I have to do the best that I can.

—**Democratic presidential primary debate,**
Flint, Michigan, March 7, 2016

❧

I just don't think insults and bullying is how we're going to get things done. And I don't think that's the appropriate approach for us. I know it's hard to imagine, but there was a time when Democrats and Republicans actually worked together.

—**Campaign speech, Futuramic Tool & Engineering,**
Warren, Michigan, August 11, 2016

❧

People have thrown all kinds of things at me. And you know, I can't keep up with it. I just keep going forward. They fall by the wayside. They come up with these outlandish things. They make these charges. I just keep going forward because there's nothing to it. They throw all this stuff at me, and I'm still standing.

—**Democratic primary town hall meeting,**
Des Moines, Iowa, January 2016

[W]e've got to get back into the habit of listening to each other and trying to get good ideas wherever they come on the political spectrum, to marshal the evidence. I do not like decision-making to take place in an evidence-free zone. I don't think that is particularly useful.

—Interview, *Newsday* editorial board, April 11, 2016

❧

[W]hen you are a woman in a very high political position, you know things that you have learned over the course of your life. You know that anger coming from a woman is not accepted as much as anger coming from a man. A man can rant and rail and wave his arms and carry on, and it's somehow viewed as acceptable. The margins for women are much narrower.

—NDTV, New Delhi, September 21, 2017

❧

It's not easy to be a woman in politics. That's an understatement. It can be excruciating, humiliating. The moment a woman steps forward and says, 'I'm running for office,' it begins: the analysis of her face, her body, her voice, her demeanor; the diminishment of her stature, her ideas, her accomplishments, her integrity. It can be unbelievably cruel.

—*What Happened*

You know, when I was secretary of state, I came out of that job I think with a sixty-nine percent approval rating, because I was in service to my country, I was in service to our president. I was proud to do it. But when a woman walks into the arena and says, 'I'm going for this myself,' it really does have a dramatic effect on how people perceive."

—Interview with Savannah Guthrie and Matt Lauer,
The Today Show, September 13, 2017

[B]efore we are Republicans or Democrats, liberals or conservatives, or any of the other labels that divide us as often as define us, we are Americans, all with a personal stake in our country.

—*Hard Choices*

FIRST LADY

Our lives are a mixture of different roles. Most of us are doing the best we can to find whatever the right balance is . . . For me, that balance is family, work, and service.

—**During Bill Clinton's 1992 presidential campaign**

❧

It was a very difficult experience, but it was the right thing to do. It laid the groundwork for what I hope will be a lasting, major accomplishment of this administration. But it had so much less to do with me than the fact that I was willing to take on a hard issue.

—**Referring to 1993 Clinton health care plan, "Hillary Clinton: Myth and Reality," *Harper's Bazaar*, February 14, 2011**

❧

I never expected that the way I defined my role as First Lady would generate so much controversy and confusion. In my own mind, I was traditional in some ways and not in others. I cared about the food I served our guests, and I also wanted to improve the delivery of health care for all Americans. To me, there was nothing incongruous about my interests and activities.

—***Living History***

We need a new definition of civil society which answers the unanswerable questions posed by both the market forces and the governmental ones as to how we can have a society that fills us up again and makes us feel that we are part of something bigger than ourselves.

—**Advocating for health care reform as First Lady,
University of Texas at Austin, April 6, 1993**

∽

Eight million kids every year have health insurance because, when I was First Lady, I worked with Democrats and Republicans to create the children's health insurance program. Hundreds of thousands of kids now have a chance to be adopted because I worked to change our adoption and foster care system.

—**Second presidential debate, Washington University,
St. Louis, October 9, 2016**

∽

Now it is time to act on behalf of women everywhere. If we take bold steps to better the lives of women, we will be taking bold steps to better the lives of children and families too. . . . As long as discrimination and inequities remain so commonplace everywhere in the world—as long as girls and women are valued less, fed less, fed last, overworked, underpaid, not schooled, subjected to violence in and out of their homes—the potential of the human family to create a peaceful, prosperous world will not be realized.

—**Speech as First Lady, United Nations Fourth World
Conference on Women, Beijing, September 5, 1995**

The First Lady role is really difficult. It has no job description. . . . You have to create it for yourself.

—*"Hillary's Last Chance,"* Esquire, *January 29, 2007*

I'd like to share with you some of the convictions I've developed over a lifetime—not only as an advocate and a citizen but as a mother, daughter, sister, and wife—about what our children need from us and what we owe to them. . . . Whether or not you agree with me, I hope it promotes an honest conversation among us.

—*It Takes a Village*

I loved it. I really felt privileged to do it. I learned more than I ever learned in my life. But it's a very hard position to be in. As a senator, it's very difficult and challenging, but it has a job description that goes with it. There are certain things you know you need to do day by day. There is no typical day in a First Lady's life. That made it hard.

—"Hillary's Last Chance,"
Esquire, January 29, 2007

FOREIGN POLICY

Well, let's be clear: Withdrawal is not defeat. Defeat is keeping troops in Iraq for 100 years.

—Campaign speech on her foreign-policy agenda,
George Washington University, March 17, 2008

❧

President Kennedy once said that engaging the world to meet the threats we face was the greatest adventure of our century. Well, Mr. President-elect, I am proud to join you on what will be a difficult and exciting adventure in this new century. And may God bless you and all who serve with you and our great country.

—Accepting position of secretary of state,
Chicago, December 1, 2008

❧

One of my goals upon becoming Secretary of State was to take diplomacy out of capitals, out of government offices, into the media, into the streets of countries. So from the very beginning in February of 2009 I have tried to combine the necessary diplomacy of government meetings, of creating structures in which we enhance our participation government-to-government with people-to-people diplomacy.

—"Q&A: Hillary Clinton on Libya, China, the Middle East
and Barack Obama," *Time*, October 27, 2011

With every tough message that I deliver, it is embedded in a much broader context. It's not, "You're with us or against us." It is, "We have a lot of business to do."

—**"How Hillary Found Her Groove,"** *Newsweek*, April 22, 2010

[T]he United States can't solve all of the problems in the world. But the problems in the world can't be solved without the United States. And therefore, we have to husband our resources, among which is this incredibly valuable asset of global leadership, and figure out how we can best deploy it.

—**"Hillary Clinton's Last Tour as a Rock-Star Diplomat,"**
New York Times Magazine, June 27, 2012

Like President Obama, I do not believe that we should again have 100,000 American troops in combat in the Middle East. That is just not the smart move to make here. If we have learned anything from fifteen years of war in Iraq and Afghanistan, it's that local people and nations have to secure their own communities. We can help them, and we should, but we cannot substitute for them.

—**Campaign speech on ISIS and terrorism, Council on Foreign Relations,**
Washington, D.C., November 19, 2015

Simply put, we have to be smart about how we use our power.
Not because we have less of it—indeed, the might of our military,
the size of our economy, the influence of our diplomacy, and the
creative energy of our people remain unrivaled. No, it's because
as the world has changed, so too have the levers of power that
can most effectively shape international affairs.

—Farewell speech as secretary of state, Council on Foreign Relations,
Washington, D.C., February 1, 2013

It is time to begin a new phase and intensify and broaden our
efforts to smash the would-be caliphate and deny ISIS control
of territory in Iraq and Syria. . . . A key obstacle standing in
the way is a shortage of good intelligence about ISIS and its
operations, so we need an immediate intelligence surge in the
region, including technical assets, Arabic speakers with deep
expertise in the Middle East, and even closer partnership with
regional intelligence services.

—Campaign speech on ISIS and terrorism, Council on Foreign Relations,
Washington, D.C., November 19, 2015

I would imagine I've thought more about what happened than
all of you put together. I've lost more sleep than all of you put
together.

—Testimony before the House Select Committee on
2012 Benghazi, Libya, attack, October 22, 2015

[W]hen I was secretary of state I did urge, along with the Department of Defense and the CIA, that we seek out, vet, and train and arm Syrian opposition figures so that they could defend themselves against Assad. The president said no. Now, that's how it works. People who work for the president make recommendations, and then the president makes the decision.

—**Democratic presidential primary debate,
Brooklyn, New York, April 14, 2016**

❧

We are not at war with Islam, and it is a mistake, and it plays into the hands of the terrorists, to act as though we are.

—**Second presidential debate,
Washington University, St. Louis, October 9, 2016**

❧

When I was secretary of state, we worked closely with our allies Japan and South Korea to respond to this threat, including by creating a missile defense system that stands ready to shoot down a North Korean warhead, should its leaders ever be reckless enough to launch one at us. The technology is ours. Key parts of it are located on Japanese ships. All three countries contributed to it. And this month, all three of our militaries will run a joint drill to test it. That's the power of allies.

—**Campaign speech on national security,
San Diego, June 2, 2016**

Our relationship with China is one of the most complicated, as we need to balance efforts to contain Chinese aggression in the global economy . . . with the need to cooperate on issues of shared importance, like climate change and global health.

—*Stronger Together*

I have been involved, both as First Lady with my husband's efforts, as a senator supporting the efforts that even the Bush administration was undertaking, and as secretary of state for President Obama, I'm the person who held the last three meetings between the president of the Palestinian Authority and the prime minister of Israel. There were only four of us in the room, Netanyahu, Abbas, George Mitchell, and me. . . . And I believe that as president I will be able to continue to make progress and get an agreement that will be fair both to the Israelis and the Palestinians without ever, ever undermining Israel's security.

—**Democratic presidential primary debate,**
Brooklyn, New York, April 14, 2016

We've never had a foreign government trying to interfere in our election. We have seventeen—seventeen—intelligence agencies, civilian and military, who have all concluded that these espionage attacks, these cyberattacks, come from the highest levels of the Kremlin. And they are designed to influence our election. I find that deeply disturbing.

—**Final presidential debate, University of Nevada, Las Vegas,**
October 20, 2016

Well, it concerns me that the deep well of experience and expertise that our country has to offer, our foreign service has to offer, that outside experts have to offer is largely being disregarded. . . . [W]e are not engaging in state craft the way we need to. . . . [T]eams need to be led by people who understand the history and how we got to where we are in order to make progress.

—*Anderson Cooper 360*, CNN,
September 13, 2017

∽

Retreat is not an option. From fighting international terrorism to combating climate change to stopping human trafficking, no one nation can solve all of these problems alone. We have to work together—and the United States must lead.

—*Stronger Together*

THE 2016 PRESIDENTIAL ELECTION

But at the end of the day, being the first woman president can only take you so far. What have I done that can actually produce positive results in somebody's life? Do we have more jobs? Are people's incomes going up? Have we made progress on the minimum wage? What have we gotten done on equal pay? What are we doing on early childhood? I'm still a results-oriented kind of person, because that's what I think matters to people.

—"Hillary Clinton vs. Herself," *New York*, May 30, 2016

Tonight's victory is not about one person. It belongs to generations of women and men who struggled and sacrificed and made this moment possible. In our country, it started right here in New York, a place called Seneca Falls, in 1848, where a small but determined group of women and men came together with the idea that women deserved equal rights, and they set it forth in something called the Declaration of Sentiments, and it was first time in human history that that kind of declaration occurred.

—Victory speech as presumptive Democratic presidential nominee,
Brooklyn, New York, June 7, 2016

America is once again at a moment of reckoning. Powerful forces are threatening to pull us apart. Bonds of trust and respect are fraying. And just as with our founders, there are no guarantees. It truly is up to us. We have to decide whether we will all work together so we can all rise together.

—Acceptance speech, Democratic National Convention,
Philadelphia, July 28, 2016

Bernie, your campaign inspired millions of Americans, particularly the young people who threw their hearts and souls into our primary. And to all of your supporters here and around the country, I want you to know: I've heard you. Your cause is our cause.

—**Speaking to primary candidate Senator Bernie Sanders during acceptance speech, Democratic National Convention, Philadelphia, July 28, 2016**

∽

I think Donald just criticized me for preparing for this debate. And, yes, I did. You know what else I prepared for? I prepared to be president. And I think that's a good thing.

—**First presidential debate, Hofstra University, September 26, 2016**

∽

As soon as he travels to 112 countries and negotiates a peace deal, a cease fire, a release of dissidents, an opening of new opportunities in nations around the world, or even spends eleven hours testifying in front of a congressional committee, he can talk to me about stamina. . . ."

—**Referring to Donald Trump in first presidential debate, Hofstra University, September 26, 2016**

There is a persistent, organized effort to misrepresent my record, and I don't appreciate that, and I feel sorry for a lot of the young people who are fed this list of misrepresentations.

—**"Hillary Clinton Has Had Enough of Bernie Sanders,"**
Politico, **April 6, 2016**

∾

Donald Trump's ideas aren't just different. They are dangerously incoherent. They're not even really ideas, just a series of bizarre rants, personal feuds, and outright lies.

—**Campaign speech on national security,**
San Diego, June 2, 2016

∾

I will leave it to the psychiatrists to explain his affection for tyrants.

—**Campaign speech on national security,**
San Diego, June 2, 2016

∾

[T]o be grossly generalistic, you could put half of Trump's supporters into what I call the basket of deplorables.

—**Remarks at campaign fundraiser, New York City,**
September 9, 2016

A man who can be provoked by a tweet should not have his fingers anywhere near the nuclear codes.

—**First United States presidential debate,
Hofstra University, September 26, 2016**

❧

I think it's clear to anyone who heard it that it represents exactly who he is, because we've seen this throughout the campaign. We have seen him insult women. We've seen him rate women on their appearance, ranking them from one to ten. We've seen him embarrass women on TV and on Twitter. We saw him after the first debate. It's been nearly a week, denigrating a former Miss Universe in the harshest, most personal terms. So, yes, this is who Donald Trump is.

—**Second presidential debate, Washington University, St. Louis,
October 9, 2016**

❧

On the day when I was in the situation room monitoring the raid that brought Osama bin Laden to justice, [Donald Trump] was hosting *The Celebrity Apprentice*. So, I'm happy to compare my thirty years of experience, what I've done for this country, trying to help in every way I could, especially kids and families, get ahead and stay ahead, with your thirty years—and I'll let the American people make that decision.

—**Final presidential debate, University of Nevada, Las Vegas,
October 20, 2016**

I've known a lot of the Republicans who've run for president been elected president in recent history, I didn't agree with them on everything—obviously we had our differences—but I didn't doubt that they were fit to serve as president. This election is different. This person is temperamentally unqualified, experientially unqualified to be president and so many people know that.

—Campaign speech, University of Pittsburgh, November 7, 2016

We believe in an America that is big-hearted, not small-minded. We believe in an America that is already great but can be greater if we do our part. And we believe America is great because America is good. Never forget that. If we lift each other up and not tear each other down, we can go even further. And I believe with all my heart. That's why the slogan of my campaign sums it up: that we are stronger together.

—Campaign speech, Detroit, November 4, 2016

This is not the outcome we wanted or we worked so hard for, and I'm sorry that we did not win this election for the values we share and the vision we hold for our country. But I feel pride and gratitude for this wonderful campaign that we built together,—this vast, diverse, creative, unruly, energized campaign. You represent the best of America, and being your candidate has been one of the greatest honors of my life.

—Concession speech, presidential election,
New York City, November 9, 2016

[W]hen your kids and grandkids ask you in the future what you did in 2016, when everything was on the line, you'll be able to say: You voted for a stronger, fairer, better America where we build bridges, not walls. And where we finally prove once and for all that, yes, love trumps hate.

—**Campaign speech, University of Pittsburgh, November 7, 2016**

So, while I'm answering questions [in the St. Louis debate with Donald Trump], my mind is going, 'Okay, do I keep my composure? Do I act like a president?' . . . Or do I wheel around and say, 'Get outta my space. Back up, you creep'? Well, you know, I didn't do the latter. . . . But I think in this time we're in, particularly in this campaign, you know, maybe I missed a few chances.

—**Interview with Jane Pauley, *CBS Sunday Morning*, September 9, 2017**

I think it's fair to say that I didn't realize how quickly the ground was shifting under all our feet. I was running a traditional presidential campaign with carefully thought-out policies and painstakingly built coalitions, while Trump was running a reality TV show that expertly and relentlessly stoked Americans' anger and resentment.

—***What Happened***

It was like the perfect storm. You had sexism and misogyny. You had voter suppression which, in our country, is a real and growing problem. You had the interference of the Russians. You had the manipulation of social media, the phenomenon of fake news. So, I just feel like I am taking responsibility, but I wrote this book, in part, so that what happened doesn't happen again.

—NDTV, New Delhi, September 21, 2017

I think Trump, left to his own devices, unchecked, would become even more authoritarian than he has tried to be. . . . I am saying that he likes the idea of unaccountable, unchecked power. And we've never had to face that in a serious way in our country.

—"Pod Save America" podcast, September 12, 2017

But at the end of the day it was about me. I was the candidate. My name was on the ballot. And it's one of the reasons I take losing so personally, because I think I would have been a good president, and I regret that there were lots of forces in this perfect storm that prevented that from happening.

—NDTV, New Delhi, September 21, 2017

I understood that there were many Americans who, because of the financial crash, there was anger. And there was resentment. I knew that. But I believed that it was my responsibility to try to offer answers to it, not to fan it. I think, Jane, that it was a mistake because a lot of people didn't want to hear my plans. They wanted me to share their anger. And I should've done a better job of demonstrating I get it."

—Interview with Jane Pauley, *CBS Sunday Morning*, September 9, 2017

It wasn't a perfect campaign. There is no such thing. But I was on the way to winning until a combination of Jim Comey's letter on October twenty-eighth and Russian WikiLeaks raised doubts in the minds of people who were inclined to vote for me but got scared off. And the evidence for that intervening event is, I think, compelling, persuasive.

—Interview with Christiane Amanpour, Women for Women International Luncheon, New York City, May 2, 2017

Look, I was prepared to be president. I had prepared and worked at it. And I go a little batty when I hear, you know, him say, 'Gee, this is a really hard job. Who knew health care was so complicated?' I did.

—About Donald Trump, NPR, September 12, 2017

I have a lot of experience and expertise and insight that I'm sharing with the world, and particularly with Democrats. I've got a new organization called Onward Together. I'm supporting young, grassroots groups that have sprung up to recruit candidates, train them, run them, fund them . . . So, I'm maybe out of politics as a candidate, but I'm still deeply committed to doing anything I can to make sure that we don't lose ground to this divisive bigotry and bias and prejudice and . . . favoring the wealthy and the well-connected over everybody else that I see as the agenda of this White House.

—*Anderson Cooper 360*, CNN, September 13, 2017

❧

I ran because I thought I'd be a good president and because I thought I could really make a difference, to help people. I will never give up on that. I will keep doing that, for as long as I am able, because that's what I did originally before I was ever in politics, before my husband was ever president, and it's what I will keep doing.

—NDTV, New Delhi, September 21, 2017

❧

I never imagined that [Putin] would have the audacity to launch a massive covert attack against our own democracy, right under our noses—and that he'd get away with it.

—*What Happened*

This loss hurts. But please never stop believing that fighting for what's right is worth it.

RELIGION

In the world in which I'm living now, there is so much emphasis on the short term and the secular, I feel really grateful to have some sense of faith and rooting that goes beyond that. And to be reminded that you have to try to stand for something bigger than yourself.

—*Hillary Rodham Clinton: A First Lady for Our Time*,
by Donnie Radcliffe, 1993

I grew up in the Methodist Church. On both sides of my father's family, the Rodhams and the Joneses, they came from mining towns. And they claimed, going back many years, to have actually been converted by John and Charles Wesley. And, of course, Methodists were methodical. It was a particularly good religion for me. And part of it is a commitment to living out your faith. We believe that faith without works may not be dead, but it's hard to discern from time to time.

—Speech as secretary of state, National Prayer Breakfast,
Washington D.C., February 4, 2010

Like the disciples of Jesus, we cannot look away, we cannot let those in need fend for themselves and live with ourselves. We are all in this together.

—Address as former secretary of state to United Methodist
Women's Assembly, Louisville, Kentucky, April 24, 2014

I have been privileged to meet some of our world's great religious leaders, among them Roman Catholic, Protestant, and Orthodox Christians, Jews, Muslims, and Buddhists. Despite their profound differences, each speaks from a deep wellspring of love that affirms life and yearns for men and women to open their hearts like children to God and one another.

—*It Takes a Village*

The search for meaning should cut across all kinds of religious and ideological boundaries. That's what we should be struggling with—not whether you have a corner on God.

—"Hillary Clinton's Inner Politics," *Washington Post*, May 6, 1993

From my perspective, religious liberty is one of the most important issues on the world's agenda today. It's our responsibility to think of ways each of us can further religious liberty and freedom. It's up to each of us, in the roles that we individually play, to ensure that our nation, which has been the exemplar of religious freedom and tolerance amongst a diverse population, continues to be so.

—Speech as senator, Seventh-day Adventists Annual
Religious Liberty Dinner, April 7, 2005

My faith has sustained me, it has informed me, it has saved me, it has chided me, it has challenged me.

—Washington Post, *September 13, 2015*

But the teachings of every religion call us to care for the poor, tell us to visit the orphans and widows, to be generous and charitable, to alleviate suffering. All religions have their version of the Golden Rule and direct us to love our neighbor and welcome the stranger and visit the prisoner. But how often in the midst of our own lives do we respond to that? All of these holy texts, all of this religious wisdom from these very different faiths call on us to act out of love.

—Remarks as secretary of state, National Prayer Breakfast,
Washington D.C., February 4, 2010

Faith is something I take very seriously. I do not believe I am a very good Christian. I think it is extremely hard to be a Christian. I think every day is a challenge to one's Christianity, and that by growing in faith, minute by minute, hour by hour, faith becomes stronger and deeper and bigger and opens one's eyes to greater possibilities and further challenges.

—Speech as First Lady, National Prayer Luncheon,
February 2, 1994

My faith has always been primarily personal. It is how I live my life and who I am, and I have tried through my works to demonstrate a level of commitment and compassion that flow from my faith.

—*New York Times*, July 6, 2007

FAMILY AND FRIENDSHIP

My mother and my grandmothers could never have lived my life; my father and my grandfathers could never have imagined it. But they bestowed on me the promise of America, which made my life and my choices possible.

—*Living History*

❧

[M]y mother, who was with me in New Hampshire in 2008, really taught me that everybody needs a chance and everybody needs a champion. . . . [S]he knew what it was like not to have either when she was growing up, because she was abandoned very young by her parents and sent to live with grandparents who didn't want her, so that by the time she was 14, she was out on her own, working as a housemaid and a babysitter, in another family's home. And I didn't know any of this when I was growing up. . . . I just knew she was my mom . . .

—Campaign event, Rochester, New Hampshire,
June 15, 2015

❧

She was my rock, from the day I was born till the day she left us. She overcame a childhood marked by abandonment and mistreatment, and somehow managed not to become bitter or broken. My mother believed that life is about serving others. And she taught me never to back down from a bully, which, it turns out, was pretty good advice.

—Victory speech as presumptive Democratic presidential nominee,
Brooklyn, New York, June 7, 2016

My dad, Hugh, made it to college. He played football at Penn State and enlisted in the Navy after Pearl Harbor. When the war was over, he started his own small business, printing fabric for draperies. I remember watching him stand for hours over silk screens. He wanted to give my brothers and me opportunities he never had, and did.

—Acceptance speech, Democratic National Convention,
Philadelphia, July 28, 2016

No one understands me better, and no one can make me laugh the way Bill does. Even after all these years, he's still the most interesting, energizing and fully alive person I have ever met. Bill Clinton started a conversation in the spring of 1971, and more than 30 years later we're still talking.

—*Living History*

In 1975, my husband and I, who had gotten married in October—and we were both teaching at the University of Arkansas Law School in beautiful Fayetteville, Arkansas—we got married on a Saturday, and we went back to work on a Monday. So, around Christmastime, we decided that we should go somewhere and celebrate, take a honeymoon. And my late father said, "Well, that's a great idea. We'll come too." And indeed, Bill and I and my entire family went to Acapulco. We had a great time, but it wasn't exactly a honeymoon.

—Remarks as secretary of state, National Prayer Breakfast,
Washington D.C., February 4, 2010

I remember so well when Chelsea was a tiny infant, probably about a month old, and crying all night long. And as I was walking her and then rocking her, I finally just looked at her, and I said, "You've never been a baby before, and I've never been a mother before. We're just going to have to figure this out together." And that is what many of us do every single day.

—*Remarks as First Lady, Mother of the Year Awards, New York City, April 13, 1995*

When Chelsea Victoria Clinton lay in my arms for the first time, I was overwhelmed by the love and responsibility I felt for her. Despite all the books I had read, all the children I had studied and advocated for, nothing had prepared me for the sheer miracle of her being.

—*It Takes a Village*

⌘

I have discovered, certainly over the past fifteen years of my own daughter's life, that being a parent is a continuing learning process, a humbling experience, a continuing challenge, and one that evolves and grows as your child does. I understand so much better a friend's description of mothers as "every family's designated worrier."

—**Remarks as First Lady, Mother of the Year Awards,
New York City, April 13, 1995**

⌘

If we believe in our children, we instill in them the belief that they are worth something. And then they, in turn, can pass that on.

—**Campaign speech, Rochester, New Hampshire,
June 15, 2015**

⌘

If you're married for more than ten minutes, you're going to have to forgive somebody for something.

—**Interview with Sam Donaldson, *Primetime Live*,
January 30, 1992**

Every marriage is a mystery to me, even the one I'm in. So, I'm no expert on it. At the end of the day, you know, love does not happen between two perfect people as much as we would wish.

—British TV talk show *Richard & Judy*,
July 4, 2003

And I have learned a long time ago that the only people who count in any marriage are the two that are in it. We know everything there is to know about each other, and we understand and accept and love each other.

—Interview with Matt Lauer, *The Today Show*,
January 27, 1998

I'm so proud to be your mother and so proud of the woman you've become.

—To daughter, Chelsea, during acceptance speech,
Democratic National Convention, Philadelphia,
July 28, 2016

And Bill, that conversation we started in the law library 45 years ago? It is still going strong. You know, that conversation has lasted through good times that filled us with joy and hard times that tested us.

—Acceptance speech, Democratic National Convention,
Philadelphia, July 28, 2016

I've been supported by a wonderful group of friends my entire adult life, and that's what really matters. They share my joys, they share my sorrows, they are with me and so understand that life is not just about the public part of your experience.

—**NDTV, New Delhi, September 21, 2017**

But at the end of the day, the job of raising children, taking care of your family, caring even for your parents as they age, is the most important job any of us will ever do. And we don't do it for pay. We do it for love. We do it for a sense of giving back.

—**Campaign speech, YMCA of Strafford County,
Rochester, New Hampshire, June 15, 2015**

HARDSHIP AND HOPE

There hasn't been anybody whose life has been picked apart and distorted as much as mine.

—Quoted by *BBC News*, October 25, 2000

❧

You know, I'm not sitting here—some little woman standing by my man, like Tammy Wynette. I'm sitting here because I love him, and I respect him, and I honor what he's been through and what we've been through together. And you know, if that's not enough for people, then heck, don't vote for him.

—Interview with Steve Kroft, *60 Minutes*, January 26, 1992

❧

I had never thought of gratitude as a habit or discipline before, and I discovered that it was immensely helpful to do so. When I found myself in a difficult situation, I began to make a mental list of all that I was grateful for—being alive and healthy for another day, loving and being loved by family and friends, experiencing the awesome privilege of working on behalf of my country and its citizens. By consciously reminding myself of my blessings, I could move myself from pessimism to optimism, from grief to hopefulness.

—*It Takes a Village*

❧

[M]y mother gave me the resilience, the grit, the get up and go. She told me, "Everyone gets knocked down. What matters is if you get back up."

—Campaign speech, University of Pittsburgh, November 7, 2016

When I got to work as secretary of state, I opted for convenience to use my personal email account, which was allowed by the State Department. . . . Looking back, it would've been better if I'd simply used a second email account and carried a second phone, but at the time, this didn't seem like an issue.

—Press conference, United Nations, New York City, March 10, 2015

[I]n retrospect—certainly, as I look back on it now—even though it was allowed, I should've used two accounts. One for personal, one for work-related emails. That was a mistake. I'm sorry about that. I take responsibility.

—Interview with David Muir, *ABC News*, September 8, 2016

You have to keep working to make things better, even when the odds are long and the opposition is fierce.

—Acceptance speech, Democratic National Convention, Philadelphia, July 28, 2016

Losing is my biggest regret. And losing to someone who was not qualified and did not have the experience or the temperament to be president of the United States. That is my biggest regret.

—About Donald Trump, NPR, September 12, 2017

Off I went, into a frenzy of closet cleaning, and long walks in the woods, playing with my dogs, and . . . yoga . . . and . . . my share of Chardonnay. It was a very hard transition. I really struggled. I couldn't feel. I couldn't think. I was just gobsmacked, wiped out.

—Interview with Jane Pauley, *CBS Sunday Morning*,
September 9, 2017

❦

I often quote Marian [Wright Edelman] when she says that service is the rent we pay for living. Well, you don't get to stop paying rent just because things don't go your way. I know many of you are deeply disappointed about the results of the election. I am, too, more than I can ever express. But as I said last week, our campaign was never about one person or even one election. It was about the country we love and about building an America that is hopeful, inclusive, and bighearted.

—Speech, Children's Defense Fund Gala, Washington, D.C.,
November 16, 2016

❦

It is often when night looks darkest, it is often before the fever breaks that one senses the gathering momentum for change, when one feels that resurrection of hope in the midst of despair and apathy.

—Remarks as First Lady, NAACP Annual Anniversary Convention,
Minneapolis, July 13, 1995

So, we have work to do. And for the sake of our children and our families and our country, I ask you to stay engaged—stay engaged on every level. We need you. America needs you. Your energy, your ambition, your talent. That's how we get through this. That's how we help to make our contributions to bend the arc of the moral universe toward justice.

—Speech, Children's Defense Fund Gala, Washington, D.C.,
November 16, 2016

I've had every opportunity and blessing in my own life, and I want the same for all Americans. And until that day comes, you'll always find me on the front lines of democracy, fighting for the future.

—Concession speech, Democratic presidential primary,
Washington, D.C., June 7, 2008

THE WIT AND WISDOM OF
HILLARY CLINTON

If I want to knock a story off the front page, I just change my hairstyle.

—**What she has told her aides, according to "Hillary Shores up a Shaky Base for '96," *Newsweek*, June 4, 1995**

❧

Good afternoon ladies and gentlemen, and welcome aboard the maiden flight of Hill Force One. My name is Hillary and I am so pleased to have most of you on board. FAA regulations prohibit the use of any cell phones, Blackberries, or wireless devices that may be used to transmit a negative story about me.

—**"Clinton Unveils Hill-Force One," *CBS News*, January 16, 2008**

❧

[T]here was a saying around the White House that if a place is too small, too poor, or too dangerous, the president couldn't go—so send the First Lady.

—**Campaign speech on her foreign-policy agenda, George Washington University, March 17, 2008**

❧

This is such a special event that I took a break from my rigorous nap schedule to be here. And as you've already heard, it's a treat for all of you too, because usually I charge a lot for speeches like this.

—**Remarks, Seventy-First Annual Alfred E. Smith Memorial Foundation Dinner, New York City, October 21, 2016**

Whoever wins this election, the outcome will be historic. We'll either have the first female president or the first president who started a Twitter war with Cher.

—*Remarks, Seventy-First Annual Alfred E. Smith Memorial Foundation Dinner, New York City, October 21, 2016*

Frankly, Mr. Mayor, I think your new hairstyle is the right way to go. After all, in Washington, the cover-up is always worse than the truth.

—**Quip about New York City Mayor Rudy Giuliani,**
after he dropped his comb-over

꩜

Looking back, I've had to listen to Donald for three full debates. And he says I don't have any stamina. That is four and a half hours. I have now stood next to Donald Trump longer than any of his campaign managers.

—**Remarks, Seventy-First Annual Alfred E. Smith**
Memorial Foundation Dinner, New York City,
October 21, 2016

꩜

I would be happy to compare what we [the Clinton Foundation] do with the Trump Foundation, which took money from other people and bought a six-foot portrait of Donald. I mean, who does that?

—**Final presidential debate, University of Nevada,**
Las Vegas, October 20, 2016

꩜

I adopted my own mantra: Take criticism seriously, but not personally. If there is truth or merit in the criticism, try to learn from it. Otherwise, let it roll right off you. Easier said than done.

—*Living History*

Always aim high, work hard, and care deeply about what you believe in. And when you stumble, keep faith. And when you're knocked down, get right back up—and never listen to anyone who says you can't or shouldn't go on.

> —Concession speech, Democratic presidential primary,
> Washington, D.C., June 7, 2008

Don't confuse having a career with having a life. They are not the same. And it is your life as a citizen—making a difference in your communities day in and day out—that may offer you your greatest rewards and be your greatest contributions.

> —Commencement address as First Lady,
> Howard University, 1998

It may seem impossible to accomplish at certain times in your life, but keeping a balance between family and work, work and friendship, and finding the time for service and your faith—that's the key to a successful life.

> —Commencement address as First Lady,
> Howard University, 1998

People can judge me for what I've done. And I think when somebody's out in the public eye, that's what they do. So, I'm fully comfortable with who I am, what I stand for, and what I've always stood for.

—Interview with Gwen Ifill, *PBS NewsHour*,
June, 25, 2014

Part of the great challenge of living is defining yourself in your moment, of seizing the opportunities that you are given, and of making the very best choices you can make.

—Speech, University of Texas at Austin,
April 7, 1993

You have just one life to live. It is yours. Own it, claim it, live it, do the best you can with it.

—"Is This Really Goodbye?" *Marie Claire*,
October 18, 2012

Life is too short, time is too precious, and the stakes are too high to dwell on what might have been. We have to work together for what still can be.

—Concession speech, Democratic presidential primary,
Washington, D.C., June 7, 2008

"She was warned. She was given an explanation. Nevertheless, she persisted." So must we all.

—*@HillaryClinton, Twitter,*
February 8, 2017

QUOTES ABOUT
HILLARY CLINTON

I was determined that no daughter of mine was going to have to go through the agony of being afraid to say what she had on her mind.

—Dorothy Rodham, "What Hillary Wants," *Vanity Fair*, May 1992

❧

In college at Wellesley, she was highly engaged in politics, respected by classmates as a campus activist, and seen as "a sophisticated coalition builder who provided extremely strong and very sensible leadership."

—*The Destruction of Hillary Clinton*, by Susan Bordo

❧

She had thick dark blond hair and wore eyeglasses and no makeup, but she conveyed a sense of strength and self-possession I had rarely seen in anyone, man or woman.

—*My Life*, by Bill Clinton

❧

[L]ong before she got in politics, she was in Massachusetts going door to door collecting the stories of children with disabilities. In South Carolina, she fought to reform the juvenile justice system so that children wouldn't be thrown in adult prisons. In Alabama, she helped expose the remnants of segregation in schools. In Arkansas, she started a legal aid clinic to make sure poor folks could get their day in court.

—Cory Booker, Democratic National Convention, Philadelphia, July 25, 2016

I wondered if Arkansas would be so great for Hillary, but you know? I've never told my children what to do. I had to rely on Hillary's judgment—there'd never been any reason not to.

—Dorothy Rodham, "The Rising Lawyer's Detour to Arkansas," *Washington Post*, January 12, 1993

I had watched her when she was first lady of Arkansas. I thought this white girl would come to Arkansas and play croquet on the lawn and throw tea parties. And she was just the opposite. She worked on public health and education . . . even prisons.

—"Maya Angelou: I'm Fine As Wine in the Summertime," *The Guardian*, November 13, 2009

I vividly remember being 6 and watching Hillary Clinton walk into the White House and forever change our notion of what a First Lady can be.

—Lena Dunham, "Why I Chose Hillary Clinton," *Time*, April 25, 2016

Hillary never turns her head when she's talking to someone. She is absolutely riveted. She doesn't look around . . . or divert her attention from the person she is talking to. That's a gift.

—Former Republican Senator Alan Simpson

[S]he was very strong, and he needed her desperately. He would not have been president, I don't think, without her.

—Bernard Nussbaum, "Hillary Clinton's History as First Lady,"
New York Times, December 5, 2014

∾

For the next seventeen years, through nursery school, Montessori, kindergarten; through T-ball, softball, soccer, volleyball, and her passion for ballet; through sleepovers, summer camps, family vacations and Chelsea's own very ambitious excursions; from Halloween parties in the neighborhood to a Viennese waltz gala in the White House, Hillary first and foremost was a mother.

—Bill Clinton, Democratic National Convention,
Philadelphia, July 26, 2016

∾

I had lunch with Hillary Clinton once when she was still First Lady. . . . There was something about her that drew me in. Is it politically incorrect to say that she was somehow extremely feminine? As we sat shoulder to shoulder and talked about children, I thought about Jacqueline Kennedy, and the way she drew you toward her with a soft, soft voice and then let her cloud of exquisite perfume, Joy, do the rest. Hillary was enchanting and impressive. . . .

—Susan Cheever in *Thirty Ways of Looking at Hillary: Recollections by Women Writers*, edited by Susan Morrison

Much like Eleanor Roosevelt, the First Lady she most emulated and had studied, Hillary Clinton expected the partisan attacks as a result of activism. Like Eleanor Roosevelt, she wrote a newspaper column, a weekly syndicated piece, and made hundreds of speeches, oftentimes without notes.

—National First Ladies' Library, Canton, Ohio

[S]he's insatiably curious, she's a natural leader, she's a good organizer, and she's the best darn change-maker I ever met in my entire life.

—Bill Clinton, Democratic National Convention,
Philadelphia, July 26, 2016

Hillary Clinton, is an extremely talented woman. She is a woman of integrity. She believes in this country deeply.

—Former Secretary of State Condoleezza Rice,
Meet the Press, December 21, 2008

I can tell you this: If you were sitting where I'm sitting and you heard what I have heard at every dinner conversation, every lunch conversation, on every lone walk, you would say this woman has never been satisfied with the status quo in anything. She always wants to move the ball forward. That is just who she is.

—Bill Clinton, Democratic National Convention,
Philadelphia, July 26, 2016

Hillary is widely perceived as ambitious: she must have plotted her ascent to the Senate and to the presidency. . . . Here again we face a double bind. Ambition is expected of men who hold high office, but it violates our expectations of a good woman. Isn't any individual who seeks public office ambitious—just like anyone who seeks a promotion or applies for a coveted job? But in a woman ambition is assumed to be a failing rather than a prerequisite.

—Deborah Tannen, "The Double Bind" in *Thirty Ways of Looking at Hillary: Recollections by Women Writers*, edited by Susan Morrison, 2008

I have known Hillary Clinton as a friend, a colleague, a source of counsel, and a tough campaign opponent. She possesses an extraordinary intelligence and a remarkable work ethic. I am proud that she will be our next secretary of state. She is an American of tremendous stature who will have my complete confidence, who knows many of the world's leaders, who will command respect in every capital, and who will clearly have the ability to advance our interests around the world. Hillary's appointment is a sign to friend and foe of the seriousness of my commitment to renew American diplomacy and restore our alliances.

—President Barack Obama, announcing Hillary Clinton as his secretary of state, December 1, 2008

She's smart. She's gifted. She is a leader. She is ready. She is a fighter for what is right, what is fair, and what is just.

—U.S. Representative John Lewis, campaign video for Hillary Clinton, October 2016

I was elected mayor two months after 9/11 as a Republican, and I saw how Hillary Clinton worked with Republicans in Washington to ensure that New York got the help it needed to recover and rebuild. Throughout her time in the Senate, we didn't always agree—but she always listened.

—**Michael Bloomberg, Democratic National Convention, Philadelphia, July 27, 2016**

What I admire most about Hillary is that she never buckles under pressure. She never takes the easy way out. And Hillary Clinton has never quit on anything in her life.

—**Michelle Obama, Democratic National Convention, Philadelphia, July 25, 2016**

[Hillary] is one of the smartest, toughest, most tenacious people on the planet—a woman who fights for children, for women, for health care, for human rights; a woman who fights for all of us and who is strong enough to win those fights.

—**Senator Elizabeth Warren, Democratic National Convention, Philadelphia, July 25, 2016**

It's hard to understand that Hillary Clinton can be very disliked as a politician while also being very excellent at the job of being a politician.

—**Journalist Rebecca Traister, quoted in "Hillary Clinton's Feminism,"** *Vox*, **September 27, 2016**

[Hillary] Clinton possesses that rare but crucial combination of idealism and pragmatism. . . . She embodies the principles of the Age of Reason and isn't afraid to fight against the confederacy of dunces who would undermine the principles of inclusion and diversity that America stands for.

—Kareem Abdul-Jabbar, "In This Crucial Election, I'm Endorsing Hillary Clinton," *Washington Post*, April 15, 2016

Hillary's candidacy is based on intelligence, experience, preparation, and of an actual vision of America where everyone counts.

—Bruce Springsteen, campaign rally, Philadelphia, November 7, 2016

Hillary Clinton has taken some fire over forty years, over her fight for families and children. How does she do it? . . . Where does she get her grit and her grace? Where do any of our female firsts, our pathbreakers, where do they find their strength? Sandra Day O'Connor. Rosa Parks. Amelia Earhart. Sally Ride. Deborah Sampson. Harriet Tubman. Shirley Chisholm. Madeline Albright. Eleanor Roosevelt. These women share something in common: capacity of mind, fullness of heart, and a burning passion for their cause. They have forged new paths so that others can follow them. Men and women. Generation on generation. That's Hillary. That's America.

—Meryl Streep, Democratic National Convention, Philadelphia, July 26, 2016

For four years, I had a front-row seat to her intelligence, her judgment, and her discipline. I came to realize that her unbelievable work ethic wasn't for praise or attention—that she was in this for everyone who needs a champion. I understood that after all these years, she has never forgotten just who she's fighting for.

—President Barack Obama, Democratic National Convention, Philadelphia, July 27, 2016

That's who my mom is. She's a listener and a doer. She's a woman driven by compassion, by faith, by a fierce sense of justice and a heart full of love.

—Chelsea Clinton, Democratic National Convention, Philadelphia, July 28, 2016

A lifetime spent in the searing spotlight has taught her that exposure too often equals evisceration. It's worth remembering that Clinton's public identity was shaped during the feminist backlash of the '80s and early '90s, when saying that you didn't want to bake cookies was enough to start a culture war.

—"Hillary Clinton vs. Herself," *New York*, May 30, 2016

Look, Hillary's got her share of critics. She has been caricatured by the right and by some on the left. She has been accused of everything you can imagine—and some things that you cannot. But she knows that's what happens when you're under a microscope for forty years. She knows that sometimes during those forty years, she's made mistakes—just like I have, just like we all do. That's what happens when we try.

—President Barack Obama, Democratic National Convention,
Philadelphia, July 27, 2016

She is the ultimate pragmatic politician, absorbing things from the right, from the left, translating it with Congress, doing the gear-grinding work of compromise.

—Journalist Rebecca Traister, quoted in "Hillary Clinton's Feminism,"
Vox, September 27, 2016

I will say this about Hillary. She doesn't quit, and she doesn't give up. I respect that. I tell it like it is. She is a fighter. I disagree with much of what she is fighting for. I do disagree with her judgment in many cases. But she does fight hard, and she doesn't quit, and she doesn't give up. And I consider that a very good trait.

—Donald Trump, second presidential debate, Washington University,
St. Louis, October 9, 2016

That's the Hillary I know. That's the Hillary I've come to admire. And that's why I can say with confidence there has never been a man or a woman—not me, not Bill, nobody—more qualified than Hillary Clinton to serve as president of the United States of America.

—President Barack Obama,
Democratic National Convention,
Philadelphia, July 27, 2016

CHRONOLOGY

October 26, 1947 — Hillary Diane Rodham is born in Chicago, Illinois, to Dorothy (Howell) Rodham and Hugh E. Rodham.

1950 — Hillary's brother Hugh Rodham is born.

1950 — The Rodham family moves to Park Ridge, Illinois

1954 — Hillary's brother Anthony Rodham is born.

SPRING 1965 — Graduates from Maine South High School in Park Ridge, Illinois

SEPTEMBER 1965 — Enters Wellesley College. She majors in political science and psychology. In 1968, she is elected student body president.

MAY 1969 — Graduates from Wellesley and is the school's first student to speak at commencement.

FALL 1969 — Enters Yale Law School.

SPRING 1971 — Meets Bill Clinton in the law library at Yale.

SPRING 1973 — Receives law degree from Yale Law School.

FALL 1973 — Begins working at the Children's Defense Fund in Cambridge, Massachusetts.

JANUARY 1974 — Joins House Judiciary Committee legal staff that is investigating Watergate.

SUMMER 1974 — Moves to Fayetteville, Arkansas, to be with Bill Clinton, and accepts teaching position at the University of Arkansas Law School, where Bill Clinton is also teaching.

1974 TO 1977 — Serves as Director of Legal Aid Clinic at the University of Arkansas School of Law.

OCTOBER 11, 1975 — Marries Bill Clinton at their home in Fayetteville.

NOVEMBER 2, 1976 — Bill Clinton is elected Arkansas attorney general.

JANUARY 1977 — Moves to Little Rock with Bill Clinton, and joins the Rose Law Firm.

NOVEMBER 7, 1978 — Bill Clinton is elected governor of Arkansas.

1979 — First woman to be made full partner at Rose Law Firm. Appointed by Jimmy Carter to the board of the Legal Services Corporation.

FEBRUARY 27, 1980 — Chelsea Victoria Clinton is born.

NOVEMBER 4, 1980 — Bill Clinton defeated in his reelection bid.

NOVEMBER 2, 1982 — Bill Clinton reelected governor of Arkansas. He wins the governorship again in 1984, 1986, and 1990.

OCTOBER 3, 1991 — Bill Clinton announces his candidacy for president of the United States.

JANUARY 26, 1992 — Hillary and Bill Clinton appear on *60 Minutes* to address rumors of Bill's alleged involvement in an extramarital affair.

NOVEMBER 3, 1992 — Bill Clinton is elected president.

JANUARY 20, 1993 — Bill Clinton is sworn in as the 42nd President and Hillary becomes First Lady of the United States.

JANUARY 25, 1993 — Bill Clinton announces that Hillary will chair Task Force on National Health Care reform.

APRIL 7, 1993 — Hillary Clinton's father, Hugh Rodham, dies several weeks after enduring a stroke.

JANUARY 6, 1994 — Bill Clinton's mother, Virginia Kelley, dies.

JANUARY 20, 1994 — Special counsel is appointed to investigate Whitewater real estate project.

SEPTEMBER 5, 1995 — Delivers landmark speech at the United Nations Fourth World Conference on Women in Beijing, China.

JANUARY 1996 — Hillary Clinton's book *It Takes a Village: And Other Lessons Children Teach Us* is published.

NOVEMBER 5, 1996 — Bill Clinton is elected to a second term as president.

SEPTEMBER 1997 — Chelsea Clinton enters Stanford University.

JANUARY 1998 — Appears on NBC's *The Today Show* and suggests that the media investigate the "vast right-wing conspiracy" being levied against her husband. Hillary further claims that the Monica Lewinsky investigation is just the latest example of this conspiracy.

DECEMBER 19, 1998 — Bill Clinton is impeached for perjury and obstruction of justice in connection with his testimony about his relationship with Monica Lewinsky. In February 1999, he is acquitted by the Senate.

FEBRUARY 6, 2000 — Announces her candidacy for the U.S. Senate.

SEPTEMBER 20, 2000 —Whitewater investigation is concluded. No charges are filed against Hillary or Bill Clinton.

NOVEMBER 7, 2000 — Elected to the U.S. Senate for the state of New York, beating Republican Rick Lazio.

OCTOBER 11, 2002 — Votes in favor of Iraq War resolution.

JUNE 2003 — Hillary Clinton's autobiography, *Living History*, is published.

NOVEMBER 7, 2006 — Reelected as U.S. senator.

JANUARY 20, 2007 — Announces her run for the presidency.

JUNE 7, 2008 — Hillary Clinton concedes and ends her presidential campaign after Barack Obama gains the delegates necessary to become the presumptive nominee. She immediately endorses Barack Obama for president.

NOVEMBER 4, 2008 — Barack Obama is elected president.

JANUARY 29, 2009 — Hillary Clinton is nominated by Barack Obama to be the 67th U.S. Secretary of State.

JULY 31, 2010 — Chelsea Clinton marries Marc Mezvinsky.

NOVEMBER 1, 2011 — Hillary Clinton's mother, Dorothy Howell Rodham, dies.

SEPTEMBER 11, 2012 — Four Americans die in Benghazi, Libya, when the U.S. consulate there is attacked.

JANUARY 23, 2013 — Appears before the House Foreign Affairs Committee and the Senate Foreign Relations Committee about Benghazi attack.

FEBRUARY 1, 2013 — Hillary Clinton steps down from position of secretary of state.

JUNE 2014 — Hillary Clinton's memoir of her time as secretary of state, *Hard Choices*, is published.

SEPTEMBER 26, 2014 — Chelsea Clinton gives birth to Charlotte Clinton Mezvinsky.

APRIL 12, 2015 — Announces her second run for the presidency.

OCTOBER 22, 2015 — Appears before House Select Committee on Benghazi.

JUNE 6, 2016 — Hillary Clinton secures the Democratic presidential nomination, becoming the first woman in U.S. history to become the nominee of a major political party.

JUNE 18, 2016 — Chelsea Clinton gives birth to Aidan Clinton Mezvinsky

JULY 5, 2016 — FBI director James Comey announces that there is not a case to support criminal charges with regard to Hillary Clinton's use of a private email server during her time as Secretary of State. Comey adds that investigation did find evidence that Secretary Clinton or her colleagues were "extremely careless in their handling of very sensitive, highly classified information."

JULY 12, 2016 — Bernie Sanders endorses Hillary Clinton.

OCTOBER 28, 2016 — James Comey sends letter to Congress indicating that the FBI will begin a new investigation after additional emails are found on Anthony Weiner's laptop that appear relevant to the FBI's previous investigation into Hillary Clinton's use of a private email server.

NOVEMBER 6, 2016 — James Comey sends second letter to Congress stating that the FBI's second investigation did not reveal anything to alter the FBI's conclusion from the July 5th statement.

NOVEMBER 8, 2016 — Donald Trump is elected president. Hillary Clinton wins close to three million more of the popular votes.

SEPTEMBER 2017 — Hillary Clinton publishes *What Happened* recounting the presidential election of 2016.

IMAGE CREDITS

ABOUT THE AUTHOR

Carol Kelly-Gangi is the editor of such titles as *The Essential Wisdom of the World's Greatest Thinkers*, *Pope Francis: His Essential Wisdom*, and *Barack Obama: His Essential Wisdom*. She lives in New Jersey with her husband and two children.